Print Handwr
Workbook For Adults

Belongs to

_____

I set goals and I reach them.

I am smart, capable and valuable.

This book is organized in a progressively skill building way to help adults develop confidence to write neatly and improve their handwriting.

This Print Handwriting workbook is divided into the following parts:

Part 1: Learning the Alphabet:
　　　　Trace and practice letters a-z and A-Z

Part 2: Writing two, three & four letter words

Part 3: Writing words starting with a Capital letter

Part 4: Writing Numbers, Number Words & Sentences

Part 5: Writing Inspirational words, quotes, poems and more!

You can use a pencil or pen to trace the dotted letters and words.

Hi!

My name is Sujatha Lalgudi. I sincerely hope you find my print handwriting book to be helpful and fun.

Write to me at **sujatha.lalgudi@gmail.com** with the subject as **Adult Print** to get free printable practice sheets.

If you liked this book, please do write a review on Amazon!

Your kind reviews and comments will encourage me to make more books like this.

Thank you
Sujatha Lalgudi

Part 1:

Learning Letters

Practice your ABCs

Trace the letters and practice writing them in the remaining space!

Are you ready?
Let's go!

a a a a a a a

a a a a a a

a

a

A A A A A A

A A A A A

A

A

b b b b b b b

b b b b b b

b

b

1 2 3

B

B B B B B B

B B B B B

B

B

1 2 3

C c c c c c c

c

c

C C C C C

c c c c c

c

c

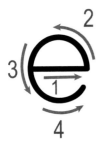

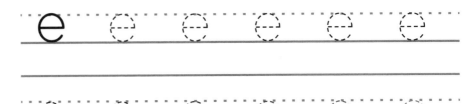

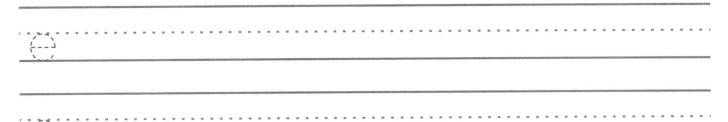

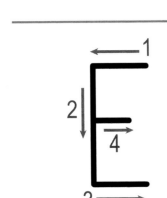

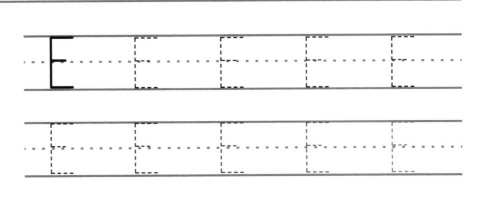

f

F

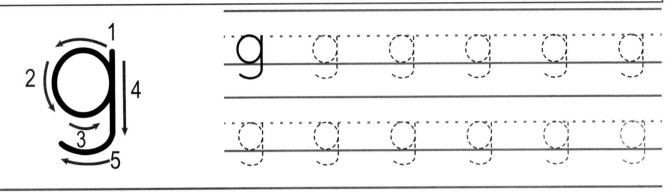

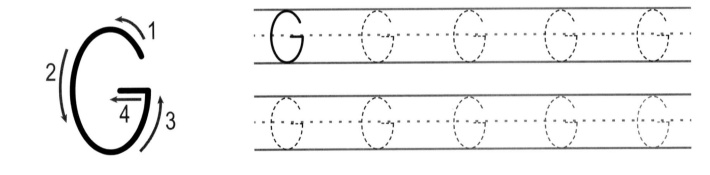

h

1 2 3

1 2 3

•2

1

1
2
3

j

1
2
3

j

J

1
2
3

J

k

K

1

2

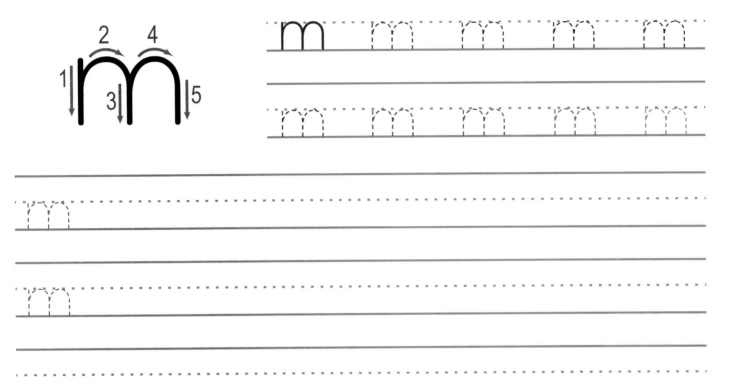

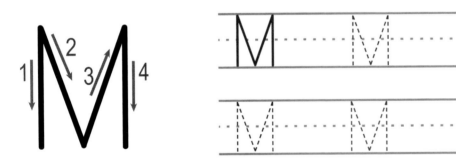

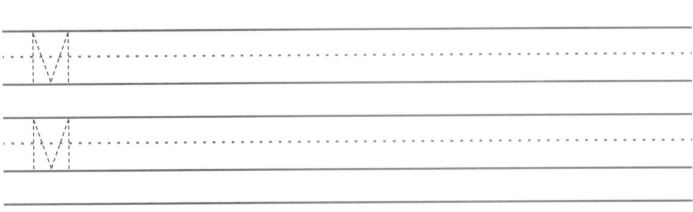

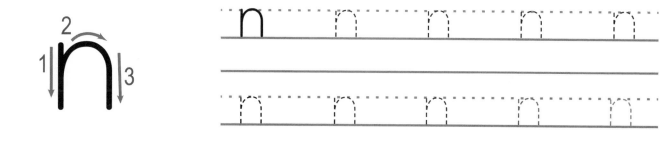

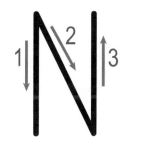

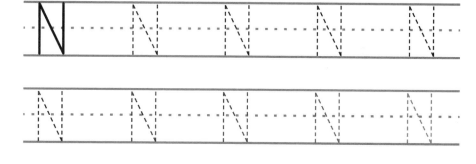

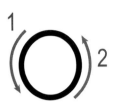

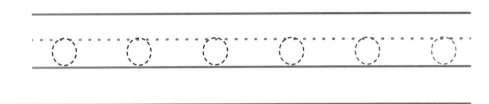

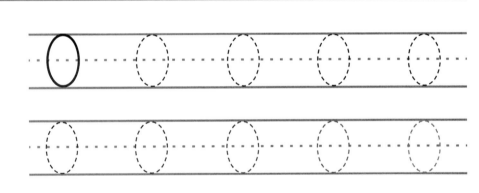

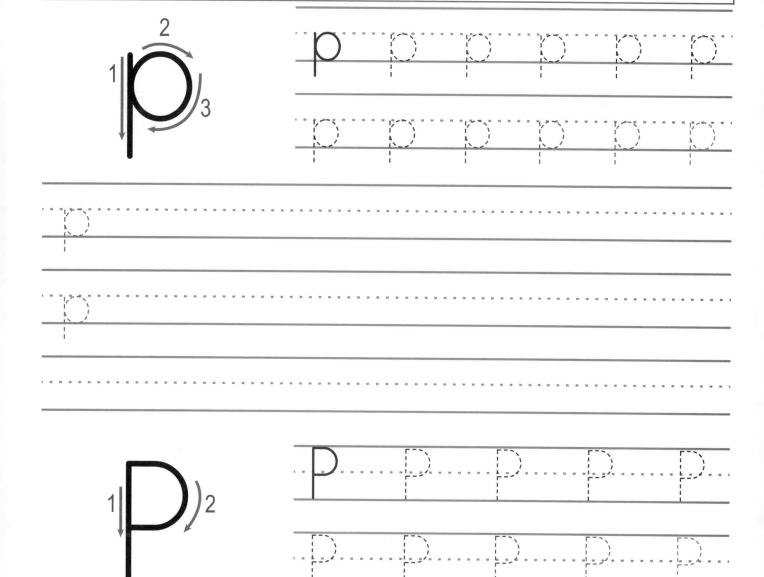

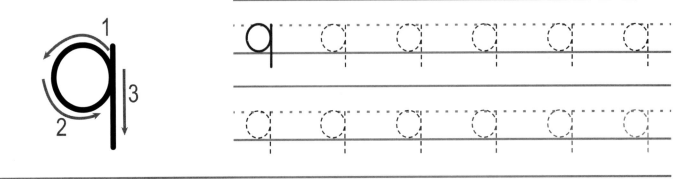

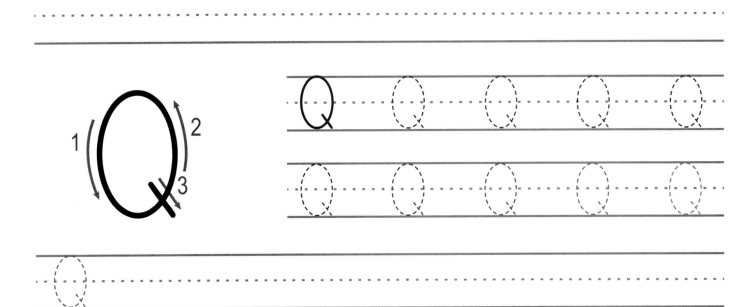

r   r   r   r   r   r

r   r   r   r   r   r

r

r

R   R   R   R   R

R   R   R   R   R

R

R

S   S   S   S   S   S

S   S   S   S   S   S

s

s

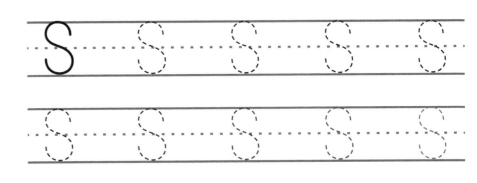

s   s   s   s   s

s   s   s   s   s

s

s

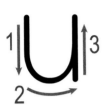

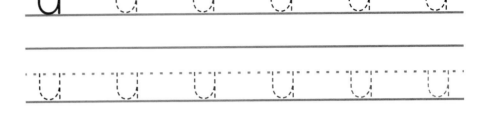

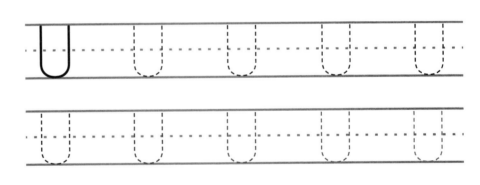

W   W   W   W   W

W   W   W   W   W

w

w

W   W   W   W

W   W   W   W

w

w

y

Y

z

Z

abcdefghijklmnopqrstuvwxyz

abcdefghijkl

mnopqrstuvw

xyz

abcdefghijkl

mnopqrstuvw

xyz

abcdefghijkl

mnopqrstuvw

xyz

ABCDEFGHIJKLMNOPQRSTUVWXYZ

a b c d e f g h i j k l m n o p q r s t u v w x y z

A B C D E F G H I J K

L M N O P Q R S T U

V W X Y Z

A B C D E F G H I J K

L M N O P Q R S T U

V W X Y Z

A B C D E F G H I J K

L M N O P Q R S T U

V W X Y Z

A B C D E F G H I J K L M N O P Q R S T U V W X Y Z

a b c d e f g h i j k l m n o p q r s t u v w x y z

A a B b C c D d E e F f G g

H h I i J j K k L l M m N n

O o P p Q q R r S s T t U u

W w X x Y y Z z

A a B b C c D d E e F f G g

H h I i J j K k L l M m N n

O o P p Q q R r S s T t U u

W w X x Y y Z z

A B C D E F G H I J K L M N O P Q R S T U V W X Y Z

Part 2:

Words

Two, three & four letter words

Trace the words and practice writing them in the remaining space!

You are AMAZING!

at at at at at

by by by by by

do do do do do

go go go go go

hi hi hi hi hi

Practice writing your own words here:

in in in in in

to to to to to

me me me me

no no no no

of of of of of

Practice writing your own words here:

pi pi pi pi pi

so so so so so

to to to to to

up up up up

we we we we

Practice writing your own words here:

aim   aim   aim   aim

big big big big big

cat cat cat cat cat

den den den den

eat eat eat eat eat

Write your own words here:

fan fan fan fan fan

get get get get get

had had had had

ire ire ire ire ire

jet jet jet jet jet

Write your own words here:

kit kit kit kit kit

led led led led led

map map map map

not not not not not

off off off off off

Write your own words here:

par par par par

run run run run

sap sap sap sap

tug tug tug tug

use use use use

Write your own words here:

van   van   van   van

wit   wit   wit   wit

yet   yet   yet   yet

zip   zip   zip   zip

Write your own words here:

able able able able

blue blue blue blue

crow crow crow crow

dear dear dear dear

even even even even

Write your own words here:

fare fare fare fare

glad glad glad glad

hard hard hard hard

idea idea idea idea

joke joke joke joke

Write your own words here:

know kind kind kind

last last last last

main main main

neck neck neck neck

over over over over

Write your own words here:

perk perk perk perk

quay quay quay quay

roam roam roam roam

sure sure sure sure

tame tame tame tame

Write your own words here:

user user user user

vain vain vain vain

want want want want

xmas xmas xmas

year year year year

zoom zoom zoom

Part 3:

Capitalization

Trace the dotted words,
then practice writing them on your own
in the remaining space.

You are
AWESOME!

Am   Am   Am   Am

Bar   Bar   Bar   Bar

Cap   Cap   Cap   Cap

Dab   Dab   Dab   Dab

Eat   Eat   Eat   Eat

Write your own words here:

Fan Fan Fan Fan

Gap Gap Gap Gap

Hat Hat Hat Hat

Ink Ink Ink Ink

Jet Jet Jet Jet

Write your own words here:

Kit   Kit   Kit   Kit

Lip   Lip   Lip   Lip

Men   Men   Men   Men

Nab   Nab   Nab   Nab

One   One   One   One

Write your own words here:

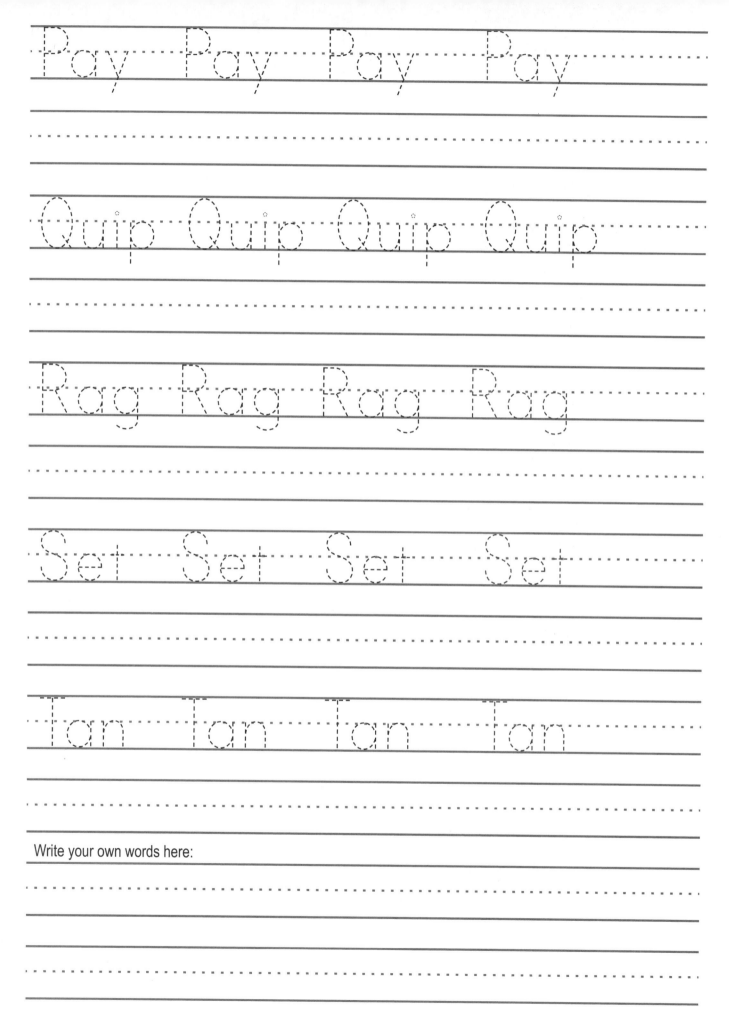

Pay Pay Pay Pay

Quip Quip Quip Quip

Rag Rag Rag Rag

Set Set Set Set

Tan Tan Tan Tan

Write your own words here:

Use Use Use Use

Vast Vast Vast Vast

Win Win Win Win

Xenon Xenon Xenon

Yap Yap Yap Yap

Zoom Zoom Zoom

Part 4:

Numbers, Number Words, Calendar Words & Sentences

We will now practice writing using a smaller letter size.

Trace the dotted numbers, words, affirmations, & pangrams and practice writing them on your own.

Use your best handwriting!

Great Going!

11 12 13 14 15 16 17 18
19 20 21 22 23 24 25 26
27 28 29 30 31 32 33 34
35 36 37 38 39 40 41 42
43 44 45 46 47 48 49 50
51 52 53 54 55 56 57 58
59 60 61 62 63 64 65 66
67 68 69 70 71 72 73 74
75 76 77 78 79 80 81 82
83 84 85 86 87 88 89 90
91 92 93 94 95 96 97 98
99 100

One One One One One One

Two Two Two Two Two Two

Three Three Three Three

Four Four Four Four Four

Five Five Five Five Five

Six Six Six Six Six Six

Seven Seven Seven Seven

Eight Eight Eight Eight Eight

Nine Nine Nine Nine Nine

Ten Ten Ten Ten Ten Ten

One Two Three Four Five Six

Seven Eight Nine Ten

One Two Three Four Five Six

Seven Eight Nine Ten

One Two Three Four Five Six

Seven Eight Nine Ten

Ten Twenty Thirty Forty

Fifty Sixty Seventy Eighty

Ninety Hundred

Ten Twenty Thirty Forty

Fifty Sixty Seventy Eighty

Ninety Hundred

Ten Twenty Thirty Forty
Fifty Sixty Seventy Eighty
Ninety Hundred
Ten Twenty Thirty Forty
Fifty Sixty Seventy Eighty
Ninety Hundred

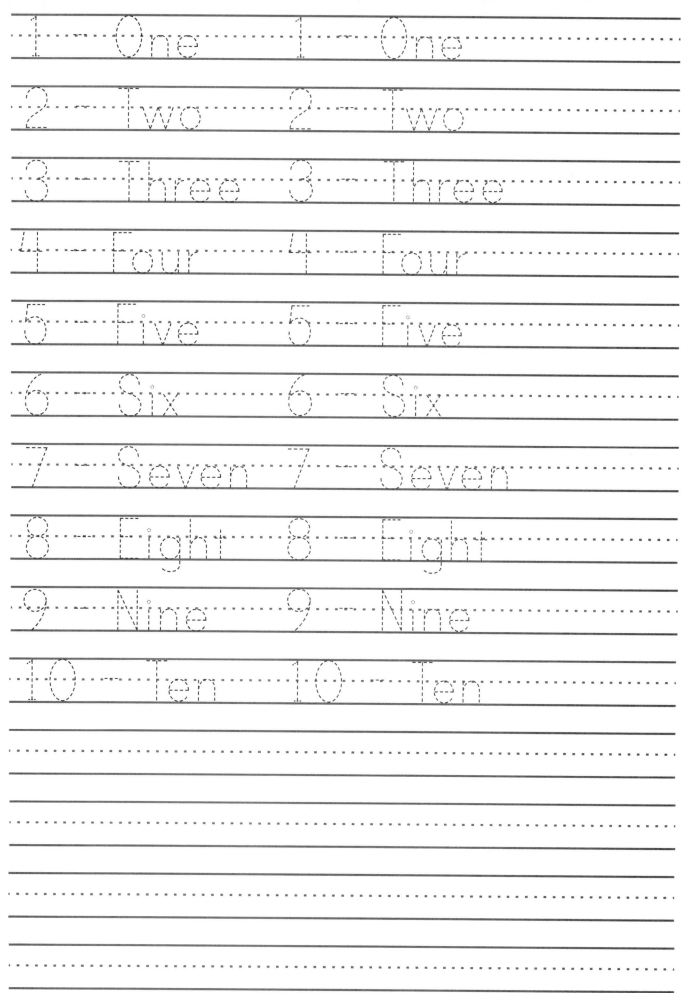

1 — One   1 — One

2 — Two   2 — Two

3 — Three   3 — Three

4 — Four   4 — Four

5 — Five   5 — Five

6 — Six   6 — Six

7 — Seven   7 — Seven

8 — Eight   8 — Eight

9 — Nine   9 — Nine

10 — Ten   10 — Ten

11 — Eleven

12 — Twelve

13 — Thirteen

14 — Fourteen

15 — Fifteen

16 — Sixteen

17 — Seventeen

18 — Eighteen

19 — Nineteen

20 — Twenty

Monday Monday

Monday

Tuesday Tuesday

Tuesday

Wednesday Wednesday

Wednesday

Thursday Thursday

Thursday

Friday Friday

Friday

Saturday Saturday

Saturday

Sunday Sunday

Sunday

Days of the Week

Days of the week

Monday Tuesday Wednesday

Thursday Friday Saturday

Sunday

Days of the week

Monday Tuesday Wednesday

Thursday Friday Saturday

Sunday

January January January

January

February February February

February

March March March

March

April April April

April

May May May

May

June June June

June

July July July

July

August August August

August

September September

September

October October October

October

November November

November

December December

December

Months of the year

January February

March April May

June July August

September October

November December

Day Day

Week Week

Month Month

Year Year

Leap Year Leap Year

Date Date

Time Time

Days Days

Days

Weeks Weeks

Weeks

Months Months

Months

Years Years

Years

Decades Decades

Decades

Centuries Centuries

Centuries

Millennia Millennia

Millennia

Seconds Seconds

Seconds

Minutes Minutes

Minutes

Hours Hours

Hours

Days Days

Days

The quick brown fox jumps
over a lazy dog.

How quickly daft jumping
zebras vex.

Sphinx of black quartz, judge
my vow!

Write your own Pangram here:

Pangram: A pangram is a sentence that contains every letter of the alphabet at least once. Practice these fun lines.

The five boxing wizards jump quickly.

Both fickle dwarves jinx my pig quiz.

Fix problem quickly with galvanized jets.

Write your own Pangram here:

Pangram: A pangram is a sentence that contains every letter of the alphabet at least once. Practice these fun lines.

How vexingly quick daft zebras jump!

Two driven jocks help fax my big quiz.

The jay, pig, fox, zebra and my wolves quack!

Write your own Pangram here:

Pangram: A pangram is a sentence that contains every letter of the alphabet at least once. Practice these fun lines.

I am worthy of greatness.

I live each day to the fullest.

I can get through anything.

I don't need to be perfect.

I set goals and I reach them.

I am my own superhero.

I can make a difference.

Trace and Copy the sentence using your best handwriting.

I am proud of my own

success.

I have courage and

confidence.

I love and enjoy everything

I do.

I am smart, capable and
valuable.

Today, I will walk through
my fears.

My potential to succeed is
infinite.

Trace and Copy the sentence using your best handwriting.

Part 5:
Inspirational

We will now practice writing
using a smaller letter size.

Trace the famous quotes, poems, play and a
speech and then practice writing them
on your own.

Use your best handwriting!

You are
brilliant!

"The journey of a thousand miles
begins with one step." — Lao Tzu

"Action is the foundational key to
all success." — Pablo Picasso

"Make each day your masterpiece."
— John Wooden

"Success occurs when opportunity
meets preparation." — Zig Ziglar

Practice writing these quotes.

"We are what we repeatedly do.
Excellence, then, is not an act,
but a habit." — Aristotle

"Give every day the chance to
become the most beautiful day
of your life." — Mark Twain

"Don't wait. The time will never be
just right." — Napoleon Hill

"The difference between ordinary and extraordinary is that little extra." — Jimmy Johnson

"Your imagination is your preview of life's coming attractions." — Albert Einstein

"The harder I work, the luckier I get." — Gary Player

Practice writing these quotes.

"If you can believe it, the mind can achieve it." — Ronnie Lott

"You must be the change you wish to see in the world." — Mahatma Gandhi

"Become the person who would attract the results you seek." — Jim Cathcart

"Begin by always expecting good
things to happen." — Tom Hopkins

"Don't watch the clock, do what it
does. Keep going." — Sam Levenson

"Well done is better than well said."
— Benjamin Franklin

"Act as if what you do makes a
difference. It does." — William James

Practice writing these quotes.

Success is the sum of small
efforts, repeated day in and day
out. — Robert Collier

"Your attitude, not your aptitude,
will determine your altitude."
— Zig Ziglar

"An obstacle is often a stepping
stone." — William Prescott

"Courage is never to let your
actions be influenced by your
fears." — Arthur Koestler

"Change your thoughts and you
change your world."
— Norman Vincent Peale

"Tough times never last, but tough
people do." — Dr. Robert Schuller

Practice writing these quotes.

"Give every day the chance to become the most beautiful day of your life." — Mark Twain

"I am not a product of my circumstances. I am a product of my decisions." — Stephen Covey

"What we dwell on is who we become." — Oprah Winfrey

Practice writing these quotes.

"Though no one can go back and make a brand new start, anyone can start from now and make a brand new ending." — Carl Bard

"Success is the sum of small efforts, repeated day in and day out." — Robert Collier

Practice writing these quotes.

The Vagabond

by Robert Louis Stevenson

Give to me the life I love,

Let the lave go by me,

Give the jolly heaven above

And the byway nigh me

Bed in the bush with stars to see,

Bread I dip in the river

There's the life for a man like me,

There's the life for ever

Let the blow fall soon or late,

Let what will be o'er me,

Give the face of earth around,

And the road before me

Wealth I seek not, hope nor love,

Practice writing this poem

Write the poem on your own

The Vagabond (Cont.)

Nor a friend to know me,

All I ask, the heaven above

And the road below me.

Or let autumn fall on me

Where afield I linger

Silencing the bird on tree,

Biting the blue finger.

White as meal the frosty field

Warm the fireside haven

Not to autumn will I yield,

Not to winter even!

Practice writing this poem

Write the poem on your own

I Wandered Lonely As a Cloud

by William Wordsworth

I wandered lonely as a cloud

That floats on high o'er vales and hills,

When all at once I saw a crowd,

A host, of golden daffodils,

Beside the lake, beneath the trees,

Fluttering and dancing in the breeze.

Continuous as the stars that shine

And twinkle on the milky way,

They stretched in never-ending line

Along the margin of a bay

Ten thousand saw I at a glance,

Tossing their heads in sprightly dance.

Write the poem on your own

I Wandered Lonely as a Cloud (Cont)

The waves beside them danced,

but they

Out-did the sparkling waves in glee:

A poet could not but be gay,

In such a jocund company:

I gazed—and gazed—but little thought

What wealth to me the show had

brought:

For oft, when on my couch I lie

In vacant or in pensive mood,

They flash upon that inward eye

Which is the bliss of solitude;

And then my heart with pleasure fills,

And dances with the daffodils.

Practice writing this poem

93

Write the poem on your own

Romeo and Juliet

by William Shakespeare

O Romeo, Romeo, wherefore art thou

Romeo?

Deny thy father and refuse thy name

Or if thou wilt not, be but sworn my

love

And I'll no longer be a Capulet

'Tis but thy name that is my enemy

Thou art thyself, though not a

Montague

What's Montague? It is nor hand nor

foot

Nor arm nor face nor any other part

Belonging to a man. O be some

other name.

Practice writing this play

Write the play on your own

Romeo and Juliet (Contd.)

What's in a name? That which we

call a rose

By any other name would smell as

sweet.

So Romeo would, were he not Romeo

call'd,

Retain that dear perfection which he

owes

Without that title. Romeo, doff thy

name,

And for that name which is no part

of thee,

Take all myself.

Write the play on your own

The Gettysburg Address
by Abraham Lincoln
November 19, 1863

Four score and seven years ago our fathers brought forth on this continent, a new nation, conceived in Liberty, and dedicated to the proposition that all men are created equal.

Now we are engaged in a great civil war, testing whether that nation, or any nation so conceived and so dedicated, can long endure. We are met on a great battle-field of that war. We have come to dedicate a

Practice writing this speech

Write the speech on your own

The Gettysburg Address (Contd.)

portion of that field, as a final

resting place for those who here

gave their lives that that nation

might live. It is altogether fitting

and proper that we should do this.

But, in a larger sense, we can not

dedicate

        we can not consecrate

        we can not hallow

        this ground.

The brave men, living and dead,

who struggled here, have

consecrated it, far above our poor

power to add or detract.

Write the speech on your own

The Gettysburg Address (Cont'd)

The world will little note, nor long remember what we say here, but it can never forget what they did here. It is for us the living, rather to be dedicated here to the unfinished work which they who fought here have thus far so nobly advanced. It is rather for us to be here dedicated to the great task remaining before us — that from these honored dead we take increased devotion to that cause for which they gave the last full measure of devotion — that we here highly resolve that these dead

Practice writing this speech

Write the speech on your own

The Gettysburg Address (Contd.)
shall not have died in vain
—— that this nation, under God,
shall have a new birth of freedom
—— and that government of the
people, by the people, for the
people, shall not perish from the
earth.

Write the speech on your own

CONGRATULATIONS!
You are a
CHAMPION!

Celebrate your Success!

Share the Joy!

Feel Great Everyday!

GRATITUDE
JOURNAL

Invest
Few Minutes a Day
to develop thankfulness,
mindfulness and positivity
90 Days of daily practice

ISBN: 1777421136

✓
Get it
Today

Congratulations

Writing Super Star
Awarded to

_____

For _____

Date _____   Signed _____